A Cat in the Throat?

A Lighthearted Study of the Contrasting Uses
of Metaphor in French and English Idioms

David Carney, Benoit Carré

David Carney, Benoit Carré
A Cat in the Throat?

1st edition

ISBN 978-1-7324567-7-8 (paperback)

Published by Independent Publisher

Cover/interior design
Mark E. Anderson

AquaZebra™
Web, Book & Print Design
www.aquazebra.com

Printed in the United States of America

Foreword

We have before us a wonderful excursion into the idiosyncrasies, the obscure corners, the mysteries, the peculiarities, the illogic (and sometimes the logic), of two major languages, English and French. The focus is on the use of metaphor in idioms, which turns out to be a productive and absorbing entry into an exploration of what matters most in any language: the communication of meaning. It is a truism that all languages are efficient in conveying meaning, but the different ways this is accomplished, as can be seen here, is a source of endless fascination. Does culture determine language, as Benjamin Whorf proposed? We don't have to be dogmatic Whorfians to acknowledge that there are indeed differences in how Francophones and Anglophones get around to expressing similar concepts and ideas, and, as we see here, these differences are not infrequently a source of delight and amusement ("a cat in the throat" being a prize specimen). In this book we are led down a series of stimulating byways, conducted by informed and genial guides, and emerge at the end of the journey both delighted and instructed.

Thomas H. Bestul
University of Illinois at Chicago, emeritus

Sources

There were numerous sources consulted in writing this study; the following were among the most significant. An asterisk (*) indicates that the source is a web site.

Harper Collins Robert French College Dictionary (HCR)

Les expressions françaises décortiquées (LEFD)*
https://www.expressio.fr/

Morris Dictionary of Word and Phrase Origins (MOR)

Webster's New World Dictionary of the American Language (WEB)

College French English Dictionary (CFED)*

The Oxford English Dictionary (OED)

Wikipedia (WIK)*

John Ciardi: A Browser's Dictionary (ABD)

The Phrase Finder (TPF)* https://www.phrases.org.uk

Grammarophobia* https://www.grammarphobia.com

Merde: The REAL French You Were Never Taught at School (MER)

2001 French and English Idioms (2001)

101 French Idioms (101)

English Language & Usage Stack Exchange*
https://english.stackexchange.com (ELU)

In Plain English: 2000 Idioms Norwegian/English/German/French (IPE)

Le monde du français* https://lemondedufrancais.com/2012/01/07/ (MF)

The Straight Dope* https://www.straightdope.com (SD)

World Wide Words* http://www.worldwidewords.org (WWW)

Word Histories* https://wordhistories.net (WH)

The Word Detective* http://www.word-detective.com (WD)

Acknowledgments

We gratefully thank Thomas Bestul, Eric Calderon, Eido Frances Carney, James Christy, Dale DeLetis. Owen Korsmo, Jean Skinazi, and Andrew Suozzo for their valuable comments as this volume was being written.

Table of Contents

Introduction

We can hear it now: "Good Heavens! Not another collection of French sayings? Don't we have enough already?"

Well, yes, we do, well, sort of...but maybe not. There are indeed many collections out there, in bookstores and on the internet, of French words, French idioms, French travelers' phrases, French risqué sayings, and who knows what else. Some are relatively brief, others are massive compendiums; almost all of them interesting. Together they provide readers of all stripes and shades a vast and, quite possibly, complete collection of French sayings and idioms with their English translations. So why add to the already crowded field?

Because rather than simply providing just another book with a long list of sayings and their translations, we wish here to examine more closely just how common idioms in the two languages compare to each other. Their imagery, usually expressed thorough metaphor, can sometimes be very similar, but more interestingly, can be radically different. Why should this be so? Well, as we shall see, words are slippery things in any language, and just because two words look the same, and mean the same *most* of the time, that doesn't guarantee that they will mean the same *all* of the time. And to us, this is the fun of the study and its real purpose. Because somehow, lurking in all of these fascinating and often curious phrases, might be some clues as to what makes the French French and the English English.[1]

Some Interesting Examples

We now provide a few examples. Readers who are reasonably comfortable with French can skip over this section; we offer these examples primarily for those readers whose memories of college French consist largely of

---

[1] Given the nationality of one of the authors, it might have been more proper to say "... and the Americans American," but that locution feels a bit odd. However, it does bring up the interesting notion of doing a similar study that compares English and American sayings and idioms. But that would be another book entirely. Maybe next year.

their sighs of relief at squeaking through the final semester of the hated Required Two Years Of Taking A Foreign Language.

One of the realities about words is that many, many of them have multiple meanings. And words in two languages, even when they have their origin in the same earlier, older word (e.g., a base term in Latin), can often evolve in many different ways. And the base term itself can have distinct nuances, or even completely different meanings, which makes for a very complex web of possibilities. So when comparing sayings in two languages that are asserted to have the same semantic meaning, it is often the case that the two languages have expressed that semantic meaning in entirely different ways.

For instance, the French word *pouvoir* descended from the Latin words *possum* and *potens* (to be able, powerful), and the English word *power* later descended from the French. But both French and English then evolved further, and while the two words maintained their original base meanings of *power*, users in both languages separately coined new expressions. Thus, translating *power* into idiomatic French will often involve words other than *pouvoir*. So sometimes there is a fairly exact correspondence:

Power of persuasion	Pouvoir de persuasion
Purchasing power	Pouvoir d'achat

Sometimes there isn't, but the similarity is easy to see:

Have *power* over someone	Avoir *autorité* sur quelqu'un (...*authority*)
The *powers* that be	Les *autorités* constituées

But sometimes there's a substantial gap between the two:

Power of attorney	Procuration (*Proxy*)
Power behind the throne	Éminence grise (*Grey Eminence*)

This last example originated in the seventeenth century, and refers to the secretive monk, François Leclerc du Tremblay, the secretary of Cardinal

Richelieu, chief minister to King Louis XIII from 1624 until 1642. Although that monk was never made a Cardinal, he wielded considerable influence over Richelieu, and hence over the King himself. He was usually dressed in a grey robe, and was quietly referred to throughout the court by the honorific "Eminence" that would be used for a Cardinal.

A different kind of example arises when words are used in manifestly different ways; this is where we begin to see that the thought processes of languages can be quite different. Thus, with the French word for "full", *plein(e)*,[2] we can sometimes understand its meaning easily:

He is *full* of ideas	Il est *plein* d'idées
Full moon	*Pleine* lune

But in other instances, that same word is used in expressions where English prefers a very different term:

In the middle of winter	*En plein* hiver
In broad daylight	*En plein* jour
Right in the water	*En plein* dans l'eau
To face *due* west	Donner *plein* ouest

And finally, there are many expressions where a word that seems to have one meaning suddenly takes on an entirely new identity, For instance, many uses of the French word *juste* are largely parallel to the English word *just,* both words having an essential meaning of *fair, right,* and so forth. Some common examples are:

The *right* word	Le mot *juste*
The *just* reward	La *juste* recompence
Right on time	*Juste* à temps

---

[2] As French is a Romance language, nouns, pronouns, and adjectives can be masculine or feminine; the feminine ending is generally shown in parentheses.

But it sometimes appears in idiomatic usages that seem, for the English speaker, to come out of left field:

I'm a bit *short [of cash]* at the moment	Je suis un peu *juste* actuellement (*I'm a little just actually*)
His grades *aren't good enough*	Ses notes *sont trop justes* (*His grades are too just*)

And finally, just to show that the problem exists in both directions, let's look at some simple English expressions:

I think *so* / *So* what / He is *so* nervous / An hour *or so*

Can one imagine, considering these phrases, that it is easy to figure out their French equivalents? In fact, just as a starter, can one even define the word "so"? Indeed, defining the English word "so" is a very thorny problem, which is why the Oxford English Dictionary devotes *six full pages* to defining "so." For native English speakers, we shrug that complexity off as though it didn't exist. But for the French speaker, the quest for the most appropriate French equivalent of each is a challenging venture indeed. To save the reader from having to meet that challenge:

Je croi que *oui* / Et *alors* (or Et *puis*) / Il est *si* nerveux / Une heure *environ*

A Note on Our Choices Between Similar Idioms

In almost every language, there are numerous ways to express the same basic concept, and English is particularly rich in that regard: *stage fright, cold feet, weak knees,* and *faint of heart* are all more or less equivalent to "Lose one's nerve." In many of these idiomatic groupings, there is often a spectrum of formality; some expressions are clearly casual and somewhat lower class than others that convey the same meaning. But it is usually the case that those lower-class expressions are precisely where the richest metaphors tend to reside.

For example, one of the English idioms found below is "Straight from the horse's mouth," a colorful and inventive expression. But that phrase would never appear in a formal newspaper story. Instead, the reporter would have written "From a reliable source." Similarly, one could use the expression "Not very perceptive" to describe a person who wasn't too bright. But compare that gentle phrase with the gutsiness of one of Lyndon Johnson's favorites: "He doesn't know the difference between chicken salad and chicken shit."[3]

So in many cases within this volume, the reader will find that the editors have a distinct fondness for the lower class, the vernacular, the patois, and even, as in the above example, the vulgar. We hope you will excuse our choices in this regard. If you do not, then so be it. Or said the way we (and perhaps Lyndon Johnson) would prefer...

---

[3] It is always surprising for people to learn that this vulgarity has an exact correspondence with German: Er versteht nicht den Unterschied zwischen Hühnersalat und Hühnerscheiße.

Un début simple/A Simple Beginning

Since starting simple is generally wise, we begin with a few idioms that are essentially the same in both languages. Even in these cases, the etymology of the expressions is often quite interesting. (NB: The parenthetical texts shown after the French idioms are word-for-word transliterations; they are not the proper French translations of the idioms. Also, if the two phrases are word-for word equivalents, no translation is given.[4])

Be comfortable in your own skin	Être bien dans sa peau
Spice up one's life	Mettre du piment dans sa vie (*Put some spice in one's life*)
Turn a deaf ear	Faire la sourde oreille
In the *twinkling* of an eye	En un *clin* d'œil (*…wink…*)

This idiom goes back at least to the 4th century and perhaps earlier: In the Vulgate, the late 4th century translation of the Bible into Latin by St. Jerome, the text of I Corinthians 15.52 uses this very term: *In ictu oculi* – In the beat of an eye – which the translators of the King James Bible rendered as "twinkling."

Dump someone	Larguer quelqu'un
Knock on wood	Touche du bois

This superstition is as old as the ancient Persians: in Zoroastrian practice, touching wood was a religious gesture. By the time the Middle Ages arrived, the practice was largely unchanged, though with different religious

---

[4] In terms of linguistic formality, a word-for-word translation of an expression from one language to another is termed a calque, and there are, in fact, varying linguistic opinions on differing types and subsets of calques. Highly interesting, but far beyond the purview of the present collection.

implications: Christians touched wood as a reminder that Christ died on the (wooden) cross.

Have eyes bigger than your stomach	Avoir les yeux plus gros que la ventre

To tighten one's belt	Se serrer la ceinture

Both in the sense of restricting one's self in some manner, e.g., cutting costs at some critical point.

It's not a piece of *cake*	Ce n'est pas de la *tarte* (*It's not pie*)

In both cases, the meaning is that something isn't easy.

He gave as good as he got	Il a rendu coup pour coup (*He returned blow for blow*)

I'm *all ears*	Je suis *tout ouïe* (*… all hearing*)

Have a tiger in your tank

Avoir mangé du lion
(*To have eaten a lion*)

Both phrases indicate a state of intense energy, or even aggressiveness. Although most sources agree that this French idiom is authentic, none that we could find have identified any source or origin. The English version, whatever its origin, is now strongly identified with an advertisementfrom the Esso gasoline company in 1959, which used the image of a tiger to symbolize having gasoline of explosive power in one'sautomobile.

Hit the ceiling
(*or Hit the roof*)

Sauter au plafond
(*Jump to the ceiling*)

Both expressions mean to become extremely angry or enraged. Interestingly enough, however, some sources indicate that the French expression can also mean "Jump for joy." The same sense can be found in the expression "Bondir de colère" ("Leap up in anger")

Train of thought

Fil des pensées
(*Thread of thoughts*)

The term "train" is used here in the sense of a succession of things, usually in a particular order. The expression was first used in Thomas Hobbes's *Leviathan*, (1651).

Et maintenant, en venir aux choses sérieuses
And now, get down to brass tacks

Now, some slightly more complex examples. These are still simple and straightforward sayings, and metaphor is minimal.

Time will tell	L'avenir le dira (*The future says it*)
Go up in smoke	Partir en fumée (*Leave in smoke*)
Once upon a time	Il était une fois (*There was a time*)
The brain of a pea *(i.e., very stupid)*	Un QI *d'huître* (*The IQ of an oyster*)
Rolling in *dough*	Rouler sur *l'or* (*…gold*)

In the English expression, "dough" is used to refer to money. English slang also uses "bread" in the same way.

Get to the point	Aller droit au but (*Go straight to the goal*)
I'm an optimist *at heart*	*Au fond* je suis optimiste (*Basically…*)
In his heart of hearts…	*Au fond de lui-même…* (*In the depths of himself..*)
Pour money down the drain	Jeter l'argent par les fenêtres (*Throw money out the window*)

I'm a morning person	Je suis du matin
	(*I'm of the morning*)

Brand new   Tout neuf (*All...*)

The English expression uses the word "brand" in the sense of a branding iron; e.g., something being fresh from the forge.

Achilles heel   Le talon d'Achille

In both cases, a reference to a significant weakness, and both based on the story of Achilles from Greek mythology.

Launder money   Blanchir de l'argent

(*Whiten money*)

As early as the Middle Ages, one can read of "whitewashing" something, i.e., making money gained illicitly into "cleaner" money.

Lose one's way   Perdre le nord

(*Lose the North*)

The literal meaning in the French phrase reflects the needle of a compass pointing north; if one loses knowledge of north, then he has become lost. This then can figuratively refer to any situation where one has lost his bearings.

Build castles *in the air*   Batir des chateaux *en Espagne*

(*Build castles in Spain*)

The expression "chateaux en Espagne" goes back to the 13th century, and was used in the *Roman de la Rose.*[5] By the late 16th century, Etienne Pasquier,[6] in his monumental history of France, describes the activity of building a castle in Spain as a useless endeavor, since the Moors seldom built such structures during their Spanish ascendancy. But older variants also spoke of castles in Egypt or Asia as equally inaccessible, and the

---

[5] A medieval French poem by Guillaume de Lorris (c. 1230) and Jean de Meun (c. 1275). According to Kenneth Clark in "Civilization," it was one of the most widely read works in France for three centuries, and was possibly the most read book in Europe in the 14th and 15th centuries.

[6] 1529 - 1615

expression became a metaphor for pursuing any unrealizable project. Interestingly, the English expression appears to have come directly from the French at about the same time, though without a geographical reference.

| To be fickle | Avoir un coeur d'artichaut |
| | (*Have the heart of an artichoke*) |

This delicious French expression dates from the 19th century, and uses the metaphor of an artichoke's heart as the symbol of a fickle person. Just as the central part of the artichoke (e.g.. the heart) is the place from which all the leaves are attached, so the fickle person shares himself equally with everyone he encounters.

| He is thunderstruck | Il est tombé des nues |
| | (*He fell from the clouds*) |

| Think twice before speaking | Tourner sept fois sa langue dans la bouche |
| | (*Turn your tongue seven times before speaking*) |

Both of these common sense adages are quite old. The English expression of "think twice" was regarded as "an old proverb" by the early 1600s; the French is a restatement of a Biblical phrase ascribed to Solomon: "The wise man turns his tongue seven times in his mouth before speaking."

| Have a tailwind | Avoir le vent en poupe |
| | (*Have the wind in the stern*) |

The incautious Anglophone might speculate that the French phrase had some windy reference to flatulence, but he would be embarrassed by the truth: The two phrases are almost exactly the same. The stern is the back of the boat; hence a wind in the stern is exactly what a tailwind is. An English speaker seldom uses this expression as a description of generally favorable circumstances; "It will be clear sailing" would be more likely. But the Frenchman might well use the phrase to indicate that some activity had a good chance of success.

Sleep like *a log*

Dormir comme *un loir*
(*...dormouse*)

The French expression dates from the early Middle Ages. Its subject, the dormouse, is found throughout the Eastern hemisphere, and is a rodent that resembles a cross between a squirrel and a common mouse. It is nocturnal, and is well-known for its long periods of hibernation, lasting as much as seven months a year.[7] The English phrase is at least as old as the mid-19th century: Stevenson[8] uses it in in *Treasure Island*, where Jim Hawkins says "I must have dozed a great deal from the very first, and then slept like a log."

Black as soot

Noir comme un corbeau
(*Black as a raven*)

Pull someone's leg

Faire marcher quelqu'un
(*To make someone walk*)

You're off your rocker

Tu es completement fêlé
(*You are completely cracked*)

---

[7] The animal is best known to English speakers as one of the characters at "the Mad Hatters Tea Party" in Alice in Wonderland; the French word is ultimately derived from the Latin "glis" (weasel or mouse).

[8] Robert Louis Stevenson, Scottish author, 1850-1894.

| Strong as an ox | Fort comme un Turc |
| | (*Strong like a Turk*) |

As the Ottoman Empire expanded from Asia Minor during the 1300s, the European image of the Turkish soldier was one of ferocity and great strength. When the Turks finally conquered Constantinople in 1453, this phrase emerged almost immediately thereafter. The English reference is obvious, and is virtually synonymous with "strong as a bull."

| Get the sack | Être renvoyé |
| | (*To be dismissed*) |

This English expression dates from the late 18th and early 19th centuries, when tradesmen went from job to job carrying the tools of their trade in a bag or sack. When they were dismissed from a job, they were told to pack up their tools into their bag and leave, i.e., they got the sack.

| Be in cahoots with someone | Être de mèche avec quelqu'un |
| | (*To be a match with someone*) |

The American word "cahoots" is a delightful invention. It dates from the southwestern United States in the early 1800s, but otherwise, its origin is unknown. It has been suggested that it derives from either the French "cahute" (cabin or hut) or the French "cohorte," which in turn was derived from the word for a portion of a Roman legion. In this idiom, being in cahoots with someone is to be in partnership with him; the connotation is often that the partnership is somewhat shady. Tracking down the French phrase proved to be an amusing journey. The word "mèche" (a match) can mean many things: a tuft of hair, the wick of a candle, a firecracker, a drill bit. But it can also have the connotation of "doing something by half," in other words, sharing something with someone, thus being in partnership with him. Andre Gide uses this very phrase in his memoirs, *Ainsi soit-il*: "Sincerity can also be questioned; but the game remains more subtle and we invite the reader to participate. He is 'in cahoots' with the author."

Thumb your nose at someone — Faire un pied de nez à quelqu'un
(*Make a foot of nose at someone*)

This offensive and childish gesture seems to be fairly widespread, though with minor variations. The American action is roughly the same as the English, using a single hand (which the Brits refer to as "Cock a snoot"). The French seem to prefer using two hands. (The length of two hands is approximately a foot, hence you "make a foot" at someone.) It probably dates at least back to the 17th century.

Hang your head — Avoir la queue entre les jambes
(*Have the tail between the legs*)

A figurative expression that describes looking to the ground when one has done some humiliating action. The French phrase dates from the 16th century, is a little more colorful, and is obviously based on the actions of a dog that has been punished for some transgression. This expression, and similar dog-tail expressions in French,[9] tend to be less used today because "queue" has become more commonly used as an erotic term.

Clean as a whistle — Propre comme un sou neuf
(*Clean like a new penny*)

The English expression has an ambiguous relationship with its close cousin "Clear as a whistle," which has an obvious source in the purity of the sound of a whistle. In any case, the idiom now commonly known refers to something that is either actually or figuratively spotless or free from stain. The French expression simply refers to the clean and shiny face of a newly minted coin.

Jam on the brakes — Freiner a mort
(*Brake to death*)

Both of these expressions mean to suddenly apply the brakes of an automobile, e.g., in an emergency. But each has a distinctive and odd feature. For the French phrase, although the word "mort" most often means "death," in this usage, it conveys more a sense of "harsh" or "brutal." For

---

[9] "S'en aller la queue levée" ("Going away with a raised tail"), i.e., being happy and content, and "Voir sa queue reluire" ("Seeing his tail shine"), experiencing pride, e.g., being fresh from the dog groomer.

the English phrase, the word "jam," when used as a verb, typically has the sense of wedging something into a small space; it can also include the nuance of suddenness, as is true here. But given that "jam" is also a noun meaning something quite different, this idiom provides ample fodder for inveterate punsters to suggest an odd cause of an unfortunate automobile accident.

| Push and shove | Jouer des coudes |
| | (*Play with elbows*) |

The French expression is an obvious reference to how an obnoxious person might navigate through a crowded marketplace.

| To make one nauseous | Soulever le coeur |
| | (*To lift the heart*) |

The French expression is unusual to the English speaker, since most common metaphors concerning the heart deal with amorous emotions, even when those are negative, e.g., heartache. But the French usage more closely mirrors the natural physical events similar to an occasion when bile rises in the stomach. Larousse defines the parallel expression "haut-le-coeur" ("high the heart") as "a spasm, uplift in the stomach that accompanies the urge to vomit."

| His face is familiar | Son visage me dit quelque chose |
| | (*His face tells me something*) |

La mêdaille d'argent/The silver medal

Preliminaries are over, and we can start to look at some heftier sayings, most with some interesting metaphors. To make comparisons easier, we divide the first few into those in which only the French expressions have a striking metaphor, with the English having a literal meaning. Then we reverse things such that only the English side has the metaphor. This is of value because it might shed some light on why one language wants rich imagery for something, and the other language simply expresses the same thought plainly. And we end this section by offering expressions in which both languages, though usually with different intensities, rely on colorful imagery to make the same point. In any case, we will save the really gutsy sayings, where the metaphors on both sides greatly embroider the basic concept, for the next section.

(*The English are prosaic while the French wax lyrical*)

| Dead silence | Un ange passe[10] |
| | (*An angel passes*) |

The origin of the French expression to describe a sudden and awkward silence is unknown. The above is probably a reasonable English equivalent, but others might be conjectured; possibly the phrase "The silence was deafening" captures the French as well.

| Encounter an unexpected difficulty | Tomber sur un os |
| | (*To fall on a bone*) |

This French expression dates from the early days of the first World War, and most likely refers to the distribution of rations to the troops. Those who got the first portions of meat received the more edible parts, and as the distribution got later and later, the portions of meat became less edible and gristly, hence, "bony."

---

[10] Though the reference is a bit too earthy for this publication, the interested reader can use Google to search for "Cocteau Un ange passe." At that point, if your French is rusty, Reverso Translation can help.

Fall into the trap	Tomber dans *le panneau*
	(Fall into the advertisement)

Confusing, until one learns that in the fourteenth century, a "panneau" was a net or fabric used to trap game. Only later did the word come to mean a panel where an advertising slogan would appear, hence, an advertisement.

Give it all you've got	Faire flèche de tout bois
	(All wood can make an arrow)

The French expression metaphorically depicts striving to make every possible effort to reach a goal. Another variant of this expression is "Faire feu de tout bois" ("All wood can make a fire").

To faint	Tomber dans les pommes
	(Fall into the apples)

Although there is no definitive explanation for this French expression, a possible origin may be in a letter from George Sand[11] to her grandmother, Madame Dupin,[12] in which she describes herself as being in a state of extreme fatigue, comparable to the state of apples being cooked ("être dans les pommes cuites").

That's quite a witty remark	La remarque ne manque pas de sel
	(The remark doesn't lack salt)

Pay the *bill*	Payer les *violons* (...*the violins*)

A fascinating expression indeed. The essential meaning is derived from a Latin expression: *Delirant reges, plectuntur archivi,* (The royals make mistakes and the people pay the price). It later came to mean anyone gaining and someone else paying the bill. Moliere[13] uses this expression in *La Comtesse d'Escarbagnas:* " Monsieur Tibaudier is not an example for me, and I am not in the mood to pay the violins to make others dance."

---

[11] Amantine Lucile Aurore Dupin, French novelist, 1 July 1804 – 8 June 1876.

[12] Marie-Aurore de Saxe, Madame Dupin de Francueil, 20 September 1748 – 26 December 1821.

[13] The stage name of Jean-Baptiste Poquelin (1622-1673), French actor and playwright.

| They ought to get their stories straight | Ils devraient accorder leur violons (*They ought to tune their violins*) |

| Eat *on the run* / Grab a bite | Manger *sur le pouce* (*Eat on the thumb*) |

| Take a long weekend | Faire le pont (*To make the bridge*) |

One can best bridge the gap between two holidays by taking off on the days between them.

| To be extremely lazy | Avoir un poil dans la main (*To have a hair in one's hand*) |

Perhaps a more modern English equivalent would be "to be a couch potato." The only explanation we found for the French expression is that, for someone who refuses to work, his hands would be so lacking in any friction (e.g., from a tool) that hair could grow there.

| Get ugly, get out of control | Tourner au vinaigre (*Turn to vinegar*) |

| Have a grudge against someone | Avoir une dent contre quelqu'un (*Have a tooth against someone*) |

The Frenchexpression goes back several centuries, when showing a tooth was often a sign of aggressiveness (e.g, as when an animal bares its teeth against a potential enemy). A variant expression ("…avoir une dent de lait [baby tooth] contre quelqu'un") appears in Moliere's *Le BourgeoisGentilhomme.*

| For next to nothing | Pour une bouchée de pain (*For a mouthful of bread*) |

Given the price of bread in France, a mere mouthful does not cost very much.

To sulk	Faire la tête (*Make the face*)
Burst into laughter	Se fendre la poire (*To crack the pear*)

The French expression almost certainly dates from the 1830s, and most likely from Charles Philipon's[14] famous caricature in which Louis-Phillpe's head turns into a pear. This image became widely known and discussed at the time; Victor Hugo refers to it in *Les Miserables.*

Go on foot, hoof it	Prendre le train onze (*Take train eleven*)

The French expression apparently dates from the introduction of rail travel in France during the 19th century. It has nothing to do with an actual train number, but rather is the supposed appearance of a pair of legs as the number 11. The reference is to those occasions when, for whatever reasons, an expected train did not appear, and the only way to get to your destination was to use your legs and walk. Although the expression itself is from the 19th century, the figurative comparison of a pair of legs with the number eleven apparently goes back to the 16th century, during the reign of Francis I (who is remembered for many things, but perhaps most of all for the presence of the "Mona Lisa" in France).

---

[14] Charles Philipon, 19 April 1800 – 25 January 1861, a celebrated journalist and caricaturist.

Leave the best for last   Garder pour la bonne bouche
(*Keep for the good mouth*)

When a Frenchman is enjoying a good meal, he often saves a piece of the best dish so that at the end of the meal he can eat that last delicious morsel, and thus leave the table with that best taste in his mouth.

Go it alone   Faire cavalier seul
(*Go on horseback alone*)

Although the French expression uses an equine reference, the actual source of this idiom is the popular 19th century dance called the "quadrille." The dance was a highly formalized dance that featured a number of couples, but also had solo dancing passages performed by a "cavalier seul" (a "lone rider"). This led to the more generalized use of the phrase meaning any activity performed by a person with no assistance from anyone else.

Drink alone   Boire quelque chose en Suisse
(*Drink something in Switzerland*)

This odd expression refers to a legendary Swiss soldier of several centuries ago who, presumably while in France, was unaware that the French custom is to buy a round of drinks for your fellow travelers. His unfortunate parsimoniousness doomed an entire nation to be known as skinflints.

Put something off indefinitely   Remettre aux calendes grecques
(*Put back to the Greek calendar*)

One of the many significant actions of Julius Caesar[15] was the reform of the Roman calendar. The reformed calendar, called the Julian calendar, was in use for several centuries thereafter (the name "Calendar" itself comes from the Latin word "Kalends," which were the first days of each Roman month).But the Greeks of Caesar's time, undoubtedly smarting over their displacement from being the center of the world, ignored the Roman ruling, and maintained the chaotic system in which there were several different calendars in simultaneous use, and each locale maintained its own reckoning of days. The implication of the French expression is that since no one agreed on what day it was, nothing would ever happen.

---

[15] Roman general and Emperor of Rome, 100 BC – 44 BC

To beg   Faire la manche
              (Make the sleeve)

The origin of the French expression goes all the way back to the jousting tournaments of the Middle Ages, when a noblewoman might make a gift of one of her sleeves to a knight who had dedicated his performance to her. The French "manche" eventually began to mean "tip" or "gratuity." And finally by the 18th century, the word appeared in the form seen above. Although some sources indicate that a variant, "faire la quête" ("make the quest") is used when the begging is done by street musicians, or buskers, others suggest that "faire la quête " would be used for taking up the collection at Mass.

Like a thief in the night   Sans tambour ni trompette
             (Without drum or trumpet)

The French expression refers to any activity that must be carried out with quiet or secrecy. It originally arose from the traditional military use of musical instruments, particularly drums, so that soldiers march in cadence, and trumpets or bugles, to signal different battle tactics. Hence, the military practice of **not** using those instruments for certain activities, e.g., the need to break camp quietly, would occur when secrecy was required. The French phrase was in use by the mid-seventeenth century, and perhaps earlier. The English expression is obvious: no thief would wish to be heard as he pilfers Grandma's silver.

Augment your salary   Mettre du beurre dans lesépinards
             (Put butter in the spinach)

Another indication that the French are seldom far from the kitchen. This tasty French phrase uses the metaphor of improving the flavor of spinach by adding butter to mean improving one's financial situation, e.g., by a second job, or taking on additional work at one's primary job. It goes back at least to the early 19th century; it was used in the French translation of Scott's[16] *A Legend of Montrose* (1829).[17]

---

[16] Sir Walter Scott (1771-1832), Scottish novelist

[17] Interestingly, though the phrase occurs in the French translation, a computer search did not reveal its use in the original English text.

| It's no big deal | C'est pas le Pérou |
| | (*It's not Peru*) |

The English phrase is apparently quite recent, having been in use only since the Second World War; it simply says that something is not very important. The French phrase, however, has a much longer lineage, going back to the early days of European colonization of the Americas (read: rape of a hemisphere). Peru, land of the Incas, was a particularly rich find, and the explorer Pizarro looted considerable quantities of gold and silver from the indigenous people. Thus, "It's Peru" was a claim of great wealth, and the negative, "It's not Peru", referred to something of little worth.

| Return a favor | Renvoyer l'ascenseur |
| | (*Return the elevator*) |

French elevators often do not return to the first floor automatically. Hence, the expression refers to the polite custom of sending an elevator back to the ground floor so the next passenger can enter immediately.

| Speak the plain truth | Parler sans fard |
| | (*Speak without makeup*) |

The French expression simply means to speak without any artifice obscuring the basic truth (just as makeup disguises the natural face). It dates from the mid-17th century.

| Do it right | Ne pas y aller avec le dos de la cuillère |
| | (*Don't go there with the back of the spoon*) |

This curious French expression hides a metaphor that has a considerable amount of nuance. The simple meaning is, as noted above, do whatever you're doing properly (i.e., you're using the correct side of the spoon, not the back side). But implicit in the phrase is also the sense that, by doing things properly, you are thereby forthright, you don't do things halfway, you don't mince words, and so forth. All of these are a rather large expansion of the simple thought contained in the English expression.

To be obvious	Couler de source
	(*Flow from source*)

The French phrase is quite old; its original use was to describe water taken directly from a river, rather than from a bottle or jar. But around the time of Louis XIV (1643-1715), the phrase took on a figurative sense, namely to indicate that some fact is the normal consequence of some other fact (i.e., flows normally or obviously). The first recorded usage of this metaphoric sense is from Madame de Sévigné (1626-1696), a celebrated aristocrat known for her witty letters.

That is far-fetched	C'est tiré par les cheveux
	(*That is pulled by the hair*)

The term 'far-fetched' arose during the early British colonial expeditions; it originally was a mundane description of something fetched from afar. But as the sailors began to embroider their stories, 'far-fetched' took on the meaning of something unlikely, or even unbelievable. The French expression comes from the 17th century; it uses the metaphor of pulling someone by the hair to describe using force to gain a needed end. It is possible that this concept can be attributed in part to Jacques Amyot,[18] French writer and cleric, who criticized some unlikely interpretations of poems as : "…twisting them by force, and pulling them, as we say, by the hair, in allegorical exhibitions. "

To be flat broke	Avoir le diable dans sa bourse
	(*To have the devil in your purse*)

Though it is somewhat uncommon, one meaning of "broken" is "bankrupt." This is the sense Shakespeare uses in *Richard II*, when Lord Willoughby says: "The King's grown bankrupt, like a broken man." The frequent addition of "flat" intensifies it with the notion of "completely." For the French phrase, centuries ago, French coins had a cross printed on one side. The folk belief was that the purpose of the cross was to keep the devil from entering your purse. So, if your purse was devoid of coins (meaning you were broke), the devil would then take residence there. La Fontaine (1621-1695) popularized this expression in his fable "The Treasure and the Two Men."

---

[18] 1513 –1593

Suffer a humiliating defeat	Passer sous les fourchescaudines
	(*Pass under the Caudine Forks*)

The French phrase provides a wonderful illustration of the richness that idioms can exhibit. It is taken from an event that occurred in 321 BC, during the early days of Rome, long before it could claim to be an empire. (At that time, Greece was still the dominant European power -- 321 BC was one year before the death of Alexander the Great.) The event occurred during the Second Samnite War,[19] and is sometime referred to as the Battle of Caudine Forks; we know of it only through the Roman historian Livy.[20] In truth, there was no battle, but it was a significant humiliation for the Roman army. The Romans marched themselves into the Caudine Forks, a narrow mountain pass, and found it barricaded at the other end. When they retreated back to the opening, they found a large force of Samnites preventing their exit. The Romans surrendered, and the Samnites chose not to kill them, but insisted instead on humiliating them by forcing them to be bound and then to walk under a yoke. By comparison with that tale, the English idiom is a pretty lame equivalent. Even if we had tried to liven things up a bit by substituting "Have to eat crow," I suspect we still would have had to pass under the Caudine Forks…

(*It's always interesting to see how animals figure in idioms; here are a few choice French examples…*)

Jump from one topic to another	Passer du coq à l'âne
	(*Pass from the rooster to the ass*)

Although the French expression is quite old (examples date from the 14th and 15th centuries), there is no evident explanation of why jumping from a rooster to an ass should metaphorically describe a conversation that rambles, jumping unexpectedly from topic to topic. While the English equivalent is seldom encountered as a common expression, it appears in the world of psychology, and therapists dealing with that very issue refer to the phenomenon as a "flight of ideas."

---

[19] The Samnites were ancient inhabitants of the Italian peninsula. They warred often with the Romans, but were eventually absorbed as Rome became a European superpower.

[20] Titus Livius, Roman historian (59BC - 17AD).

Bitterly cold   Un froid *de canard*
                                     (*A duck's cold*)

The best time to hunt ducks is in the deep of winter, when the temperature is at its coldest. That is when ducks leave the safety of lakes and are therefore exposed to hunters.

A *drastic* remedy   Un remede *de cheval*
                                    (*...remedy of a horse*)

There is no explanation that we were able to find for this curious French expression. It is conceivable, perhaps, that it is related to the humorous expression in English of a "horse pill," which is a pill that is very large and hence difficult to swallow, but is therefore assumed to be a strong remedy.

Get back on track /   Revenons à nos moutons
Get back to the point   (*Let's return to our sheep*)

This expression dates back to the late fifteenth century, and appears in the anonymous Medieval farce *La Farce de Maître Pathelin* (apparently a real thigh-slapper during that time). It concerns a trial whose characters are a judge, a lawyer named Pathelin, a shepherd accused of stealing sheep, and a dealer in cloth (and thus sheets). As the various testimonies become confused, the exasperated judge cries "Let's get back to the sheep!" Possibly another English equivalent, and one often used in comic situations, could be "But I digress..."

To fizzle out	Finir en queue de poisson
	(*To finish like the tail of a fish*)

For the French expression, some sources ascribe it to the classical Roman author Horace, where he compares a poor work of art to a statue whose top represents the bust of a beautiful woman but whose lower part ends in the tail of a fish. Whether accurate or not, Balzac,[21] in his novel *Ferragus, chef des Dévorants* (1833) made the same reference: "Some streets (of Paris), as well as the rue Montmartre, have a beautiful head and end in the tail of a fish." The English expression, now meaning to fail or stop abruptly, as when a lit fuse dies out before it reaches the dynamite, goes back to the mid-19th century. But an older meaning of "fizzle," dating back to the 13th century, is "to break wind quietly," a skill which, under certain circumstances, could prove quite useful.[22]

Play *tag*	Jouer à *chat (Play at cat)*

Bosom Buddies	Copains comme cochons
	(*Friends like pigs*)

This English phrase today simply means close pals, friends, or (in England) mates. But the original notion of a <u>bosom</u> friend in fact goes all the way back to Roman days, where the phrase *sodali pectoris* (friend of the heart) referred to a very intimate companion, i.e., someone with whom you would share your most private thoughts. The curious French expression dates from the 16th century. Its odd association of pigs as friends is the result of corruption of the Old French word "soçon" ("comrade"). This word was derived from the Latin "socius," which is normally translated as "companion," and its feminine form -- "sochon" is the likely route by which "soçon" became "cochon." In any case, the expression has lasted through the centuries, though the original form of "camarades comme cochons" became "amis..." and by the 19th century "copains..."

---

[21] Honoré de Balzac (1799-1856), French novelist and playwright.

[22] It might be clutching at straws, but in "Chaucer and his World," by eminent Chaucerian scholar Derek Brewer, we read "...The business details of the Italian journey slowly fizzled on..." which is a most curious way to describe business details. Unless, of course, Brewer was making a very subtle joke, using a word which would be quite well known to Chaucer, but that would be humorous only to someone familiar with the kind of earthy vocabulary that Chaucer might use.

| Hit the mark | Faire mouche |
| | (*To make a fly*) |

Surprisingly, these two expressions are actually very close. The French phrase does not concern the common insect, but dates from the 17th century, when it became fashionable for an upper-class woman to put a small black dot on her face to emphasize the whiteness of her skin (peasants who spent their time in fields would have darker skin). This small dot could, when viewed from a distance, appear to resemble the central circle on an archery target. Hence, "fly" would refer to the center of the target, e.g., the place where one would hit the mark.

| Keep everybody happy | Ménager le chevre et la chou |
| | (*Manage the goat and the cabbage*) |

The metaphorical opposition of goat and cabbage apparently goes back several centuries; the meaning of the French idiom is simply to keep the goat content without letting him eat the cabbage (which thus makes the cabbage happy as well).

It's nothing to	Il n'y a pas de quoi
make a fuss about	fouetter un chat
	(*It's nothing to whip a cat about*)

The French word "fouet" can be translated either as "whip" or as "whisk," i.e., in the culinary sense. And as we shall see, the French have a thing with cats in their idioms….

(*And now the English strut their stuff while the French show their quiet side…*)

| Sit on the fence | S'abstenir de prendre position |
| | (*Abstain from taking a position*) |

Some sources equate "Sit on the fence" with a French idiom we saw earlier ("Ménager la chèvre et le chou"). But we feel that there is not a sufficient parallel between the two. The English phrase suggests a refusal to decide, but the French idiom of goat and cabbage has more a sense of arbitrating between opposing forces, and keeping both sides satisfied. So we use the less prosaic, but more accurate, French phrase above.

| Easy as Pie | Simple comme bonjour |
| | (*Easy as hello*) |

| To be off base | Se tromper |
| | (*To deceive one's self*) |

In the nick of time — Juste à temps (*Right on time*)

In English, "nick" means a small cut in a surface, a notch. This expression likely emerged in the late 16th century, with the meaning that anything that was "in the nick" was exactly where it should be. It later took on the sense that something had occurred only moments before a deadline, with no time to spare.

When the dam breaks — Quand l'affaire éclatera
(*When the matter bursts*)

The English phrase has many equivalents – it's going to pop wide open; when all hell breaks loose; and the always reliable: when the shit hits the fan. The latter vulgar expression is messy metaphorical depiction of what occurs when a close-held or unfortunate secret becomes well known. It dates from the early 20th century, and obviously arose after the invention of the electric fan. However, we should note that the French have also borrowed the English expression almost literally: "Ça va chier dans le ventilo" ("It will shit in the fan").

Fly by the seat of your pants — Voler sans visibilité
(*Fly without visibility*)

This is one of the rare expressions whose precise origin is known. It appeared as the newspaper headline "Corrigan Flies by the Seat of His Pants", in The Edwardsville Intelligencer, 19th July 1938. Douglas Corrigan, known widely as "Wrong Way Corrigan," was a maverick pilot during the 1920s and 30s. At that time, aviation was still developing the technologies that are now required for flight, and pilots like Corrigan could and did ignore such necessities as radios or proper instruments. His famous flight occurred after he had twice been refused permission to attempt a transatlantic flight from New York to Ireland. He therefore filed a flight plan from New York to California, but after taking off to the east, he continued in that direction, landing 28 hours later at an airfield near Dublin. He claimed, though with few people believing him, that he did not realize his error due to his 20-year old compass.

Not have a leg to stand on	Être a bout d'arguments valables
	(*To be at the end of valid arguments*)

Pay through the nose   Payer *cher* (..*dearly*)

There are two theories of the origin of the English expression. One is that it derives from the British slang word "rhino," meaning "money," but ultimately derived from the Greek "rhinos," nose. The other goes all the way back to the 9th century Danes, who exacted taxes from the Irish, and failure to pay mean having one' nose slit. It certainly is at least as old as the 17th century: in Marvell's *The Rehearsal Tranpos'd* we read: "… had bought it all up, and made them pay for it most unconscionably, and through the nose."[23]

Make bricks without straw   Faire les choses à moitié
                              (*Do things halfway*)

The English phrase refers to performing a task which must be undertaken without appropriate resources; its origin probably goes back to the Book of Exodus, where Pharaoh punishes the Israelites: "Ye shall no more give [them] straw to make brick, as heretofore: let them go and gather straw for themselves" but still demanding the same output of bricks as before.

Face the music   Tenir tete a l'orage
                   (*To stand up to the storm*)

The English expression apparently dates from the mid-19th century, but its origin is unknown.

Bite off more than   Présumer de ses forces
one can chew   (*Presume one's strength*)

The French phrase uses "presume" in the sense of being overconfident, i.e., presumptuous, The English phrase likely refers to chewing tobacco.

---

[23] Andrew Marvell (1621-1678), English poet.

Get off scot-free

S'en tirer à bon compte
(*Get off on the cheap*)

The English expression is quite old, going all the way back to Old English and the days of William the Conqueror.[24] The term "scot," originally a Scandinavian term, referred to a tax, and thus the phrase describes someone who has managed to avoid paying his lawful tax.

Devil-may-care

Insouciant
(*Carefree, heedless*)

This curious English phrase, meaning to be reckless, or careless, dates at least back to Dickens[25] (in *The Pickwick Papers*), but is probably earlier. One often-quoted theory is that is originated with sea pirates, who had no worries about the consequences of their piracy; the only one who would care, of course, would be the devil.

Keep your eyes peeled

Garder les yeux ouvert
(*Keep your eyes open*)

This odd English expression began in England during the period when Sir Robert Peel[26] was Home Secretary of the UK. He established the Metropolitan Police Force with a main office at Scotland Yard; he also established the ethical behavior that police must adhere to. His police officers were named "bobbies" in his honor, and also "peelers." The name bobbies is still in use, but peeler survives only in the above phrase, which suggests that the police should keep a watch out for lawbreakers.

Kangaroo court

Tribunal irrégulier
(*Irregular court*)

What little is known about the etymology of this well-known English expression is that it did not, in all likelihood, originate in Australia. It refers to holding fraudulent juridical proceedings that have nothing more than the appearance of regular judicial practice. One belief about the expression is that the kangaroo metaphor is used to describe such activities

---

[24] William I (c. 1028 – 1087)

[25] Charles Dickens (1812-1870), English novelist.

[26] Sir Robert Peel (1788 – 1850), twice Prime Minister of the UK.

as "leaping" over (i.e., ignoring) evidence that is inconvenient. In any case, it first appeared in the middle of the 19th century. One commonly accepted explanation is that it appeared during the California Gold Rush of 1849 (in which, it is true, many Australians participated). Related to this is the parallel theory that Kangaroo courts were used to settle claims of claim jumping.

(English too has its share of animal metaphors...)

Throw a monkey wrench into the works	Flanquer la pagaille (*Toss a mess*)

A monkey wrench has nothing to do with any kind of ape, but is a particular kind of wrench, one that was used on horse-drawn coaches. The English expression uses the metaphor of throwing such a wrench into a threshing machine to describe any destructive action taken to halt some orderly process.

Beat a dead horse	S'acharner inutilement (*Work furiously [but] uselessly*)

The English expression appears in the OED the first time in 1867 as "Flog a dead horse..."

Straight from the horse's mouth	De source sûre (*From an assured source*)

The English phrase comes from the world of horse racing, and refers to a tip about which horse will win a race – who else could be a better source than the horse itself?

Hold your horses	Minute
Go to the dogs	Aller à vau l'eau (*Go down the river*)
It's dog eat dog	Les loups se mangent entre eux (*The wolves eat each other*)
What's good for the goose is good for the gander	Ce qui vaut pour l'un vaut aussi pour l'autre (*What is worth for one is* *also worth for the other*)

(*Now some gentle imagery on both sides…*)

Kiss something goodbye	Faire une croix sur quelque chose (*Make a [sign of the] cross* *on something*)
Spitting image	Tout craché (*All spit*)

The exact origin of neither phrase is known, though the English one was known by the mid-19th century. The French is a vulgar form of the synonymous phrase "tout le portrait."

Get on someone's nerves	Casser les pieds à quelqu'un (*To break someone's feet*)

The verb "casser" essentially means "to break," but idiomatically can correspond to many other English words: "Casser la baroque" ("Break the place apart," e.g, "Bring down the house"); "Ça ne casse rien" ("That breaks nothing," e.g., It's "nothing to write homeabout").

It's all Greek to me

Pour moi c'est du chinois
(*For me, it's Chinese*)

Both phrases describe hearing something that is incomprehensible. The French expression also has a variant that uses Hebrew as the incomprehensible language, and some sources also note a variant with Iroquois; the Hebrew expression is apparently the oldest. The English expression probably dates from medieval times; it was certainly part of the language by the time of Shakespeare; in *Julius Caesar*, Casca says: "…those that understood him smiled at one another and shook their heads; but, for mine own part, it was Greek to me."

Be the odd man out

Être la cinquième
roue du carrosse
(*Be the fifth wheel on the wagon*)

The English word "odd," originally derived from the Scandinavian languages in the 14th century, and generally refers to a numerical quality, i.e., "odd" as opposed to "even." But soon thereafter, it also took on the sense both of "singular" and "peculiar." It is the latter sense that is preserved in this idiom. The French expression simply observes that, given the standard design of a wagon or carriage, there is no additional value to adding a fifth wheel.

Do something *off the cuff*

Faire quelque chose
au pied levé
(*Do something with your foot raised*)

For the French expression, figuratively, if one is about to leave a conversation, and suddenly is asked an unexpected question, his foot could be raised to take his first step, hence, not be fully prepared to answer. The English expression possibly dates from the early 20th century theatre world, when an actor might have scribbled his lines on the cuff of his costume.

My jaw dropped

Les bras m'en tombent
(*My arms fall to me*)

The French expression is first recorded in 1762, and refers to those occasions where a person is so stunned by some sudden event that he is momentarily unable to continue what he was doing, and even loses control of his motor functions; hence, his arms drop to his sides. Most discussions of this idiom give translations such as "I am stupefied" or "I am amazed." But those lose the physicality of the French saying, which the above nicely preserves.

| Draw a blank | Faire chou blanc |
| | (*Make white cabbage*) |

Both of these expressions refer to a failure to succeed, and both are quite old. The French came from the region of Berry, during the 16th century in central France, where, because of the local dialect, a confusion arose between "chou" (cabbage) and "coup" (a blow); the dialect word for "coup" was "choup." And in the game of Skittles, a "white c(h)oup was a draw, with no winner. The cabbage version of the word is what has survived. The English phrase, from nearly the same period, stemmed from the creation of a national lottery by Elizabeth I. The way the lottery was structured, a ticket with each contestant's name on it was put into a large pot, and tickets with prizes (or nothing) printed on them put into another pot. Tickets were drawn from both pots at the same time. If your name was drawn when a ticket had some cash value on it, you got that money; if it had nothing in it, you "drew a blank."

| Walk on the wild side | Rotir le balai |
| | (*To roast the broom*) |

This fascinating French expression has a curious history. Originally, from roughly the 16th to the 18th centuries, it referred to people who lived in dire poverty; it describes a state where being so poor, and having no more wood, you are reduced to burning your broom to keep warm. In the eighteenth century, however, and largely due to Rousseau,[27] the meaning underwent a massive transformation, becoming a description of someone who lives a life of wantonness and debauchery. The basis of this new meaning might be that it alludes to witches riding their brooms, which are set on fire by the flames of hell.

---

[27] Jean-Jacques Rousseau, 1712-1778, French philosopher who strongly influenced the progress of the Enlightenment throughout Europe.

Have a *lot on your plate*   Avoir du *pain sur la planche*
                                    (*Have bread on the plank*)

The original connotation of the French expression was of having sufficient
resources for the future; to be well stocked up. This was because bread
at an earlier time was more long-lasting than it now is, so having several
loaves of bread on the table meant you were well supplied for several days.
In our present days of short-lived bread, the expression has come to mean
much the same as the English one.

Clean up one's act   Acheter une conduite
                            (*To buy a* [*new behavior*)

The English equivalent could as easily be "go straight" or "turn over a
new leaf."

Catch someone red-handed   Prendre quelqu'un main
                                  dans le sac
                                  (*Catch someone with his hand in
                                  the bag*)

The English expression is originally from Scotland, and refers to someone
with a bloody hand, most likely from poaching.

Open a can of worms   Ouvrir la boîte de Pandore
                             (*Open the box of Pandora*)

The French expression is derived from the Greek myth of Pandora, who
opened a box from which sprang all of the sicknesses and diseases that af-
flict mankind. The English expression is far later, probably from the 20th
century. It uses the metaphorical image of a fisherman's can of worms
used for bait to describe a situation where taking some apparently simple
action (opening a can) causes massive complications (hundreds of slither-
ing worms in your rowboat).

(*A night out with the guys seems to be similar in both languages, and often has the same unfortunate result...*)

Have a hangover | Avoir la gueule de bois
(*Have a mouth of wood*)

The French expression actually connotes "to have a headache." The word "gueule" typically refers to the mouth of an animal, though it is occasionally used, in a vulgar or insulting way, to refer to a human mouth, e.g., "ferme ta gueule" ("shut your mouth"). "Gueule" also sometimes refers to the entire animal's head. Here, the implication is that the mouth of a hungover person is anything but a normal human mouth. Yet another way the French express this thought is "avoir mal aux cheveux," ("have pain in your hair").

Sleep it off | Cuver son vin
(*Ferment the wine*)

A *cuve* is a fermentation tank in which wine matures.

Toss one back | Se jeter un verre
derriere la cravat
(*Throw a glass behind the tie*)

Figuratively, the neck is behind the tie, and hence the throat as well, which is where the drink is aimed for.

Tell it like it is | A l'emporte-pièce
(*Like the cookie cutter*)

The French phrase emerged in the 18th century as a figurative description of sharp, painfully honest speech, using the metaphor of a cookie cutter, the sharp metal implement used to cut dough.

Skinny as a rail | Maigre comme un clou
(*Skinny as a nail*)

The French expression is an updated version of "skinny like a hundred nails," dating from when nails were sold in groups of one hundred. The English is merely one of many equivalent phrases, e.g., skinny as a rake, skin and bones.

Make it snappy	Faire fissa
	(*Make fissa*)

The French expression, meaning hurry! or be quick! is pure slang, It was picked up by French troops in Algeria during the late 19th century, and became popular in France itself in the early 20th. It is derived from the Algerian "fi s-sa a," meaning "fast." The English expression arose sometime in the early 20th century, but the word "snap" or "snappy," with a meaning of smart or elegant, goes back well into the 19th century. Many other English expressions could appear in its place: chop-chop, lickety-split, ASAP, and so forth.

Fit to be tied	Etre fou à lier
	(*To be mad to bind*)

The origin of this expression, in both languages, was the practice, in institutions for the mentally ill, of tying up violent patients to keep them from either injuring themselves or others. Although the French phrase can be dated back to the 17th century, the English seems to be later, about the early 19th century. The practice of binding violent patients was abandoned after the invention of the strait jacket. The expression has moderated; the customary use now is "to be extremely angry." The French can also be translated into English as "Mad as a hatter."

It doesn't cut the mustard	Ça ne fait pas le poids
	(*That doesn't make the weight*)

This curious English expression, meaning that something is not good enough, or is deficient in some manner, was apparently in use by the 1890s. It first appears in fiction in 1907, in an O Henry short story, "Cupid A La Carte" from the collection *The Heart of the West:*

> By nature and doctrines I am addicted to the habit of discovering choice places wherein to feed. So I looked around and found a proposition that exactly cut the mustard.

But using "mustard" to refer to something one is enthusiastic about, goes all the way back to the 1600s, in the expression "keen as mustard" (to have great enthusiasm for something). One guess is that a person's zest for something is a metaphor for the zest of the spice. And the word "mustard" itself has an odd history. Historically, the word "must," descended from the

Latin phrase *vinum mustum* (young wine), and refers to a liquid made from crushed grapes, this being the initial step in making wine; this liquid is called "must" to his day. The Latin term for the spice we call mustard was *sinapi*. But somewhere along the line, when mustard seed *(granum sinapis)* started being added to the liquid from crushed grapes ("must"), the seed, and hence the spice itself, took on the name of the liquid, i.e., must-ard.

Hang someone out to dry   Vouer aux gemonies
                                (*Condemn to the gémonies*)

Both expressions describe being held up to some kind of scorn or shame, often unfairly. For the French phrase, the "Gemonies" refers to the Stair-way of Laments *(scalae gemoniae)* in ancient Rome, a staircase on the Aventine Hill, down which the bodies of executed criminals would be thrown, eventually to fall in to the Tiber. The reference is thus quite old, though a source for the expression cannot be found before the 19th century. The origin of the English phrase is hazy; we could find no source earlier than the mid-20th century.

Came within a whisker   Il s'en est fallu d'un cheveu
                              (*It had to be a hair*)

Both of these idioms use the image of a single human hair to describe some event that either barely succeeded or failed by a tiny margin.

Mighty oaks from tiny acorns grow	Les petits ruisseaux font les grandes rivières
	(*Small streams become great rivers*)

Both expressions are quite old; the French can be dated back to the 17th century, and the English even back to Chaucer. The English phrase is generally thought of as a simple proverb meaning "many small things become one big thing." But the French expression, even from the earliest uses, appears to have been a figurative description of accumulation of money.

Give someone free rein	Lâcher la bride à quelqu'un
	(*Let go the bridle on someone*)

Both phrases use a metaphor that originated quite naturally from the traditional mode of transportation for several centuries, the horse. The bridle of the horse is made up of the bit that goes into the horse's mouth, and the reins that the rider uses to direct the horse. After a long ride, the rider lets the reins go, and then the horse can walk freely where he wishes. The French expression dates back to the 16th century; we were unable to find any indication of the origin of the English one, but it is very likely from the period.

I wouldn't touch him with ten-foot pole	Il n'est pas à prendre avec des pincettes
	(*He's not to be taken with tweezers*)

The images are exuberant in both languages, and describe one's reaction to a person who is dangerous, or repulsive, or repugnant, or any other feature that would make someone untouchable. One dictionary translates the French expression as "He's like a bear with a sore head." But that translation shines a little light on the difference in the idioms' means of protection: a ten-foot pole might be useful against an angry bear, but a pair of tweezers, to use another idiom, wouldn't do diddly.

Have a millstone around one's neck	Trâiner un boulet
	(*Drag a ball*)

The figurative meaning of both phrases is that someone has a massive responsibility, a burden from which one cannot escape. The English phrase is quite old, and is Biblical, deriving from Matthew 18:6: "If anyone causes one of these little ones—those who believe in me—to stumble, it would be better for them to have a large millstone hung around their neck and to be drowned in the depths of the sea." The French expression dates from the 18th century, and the "ball" refers to the ball and chain that would be locked onto prisoners.

| To be in a pickle | Être dans le pétrin |
| | (*To be in a mess*) |

The English phrase is synonymous with several close cousins – be in a fix, be in a stew – and goes at least back to Shakespeare. Its origin is disputed, but probably is a sideways reference to the process of stewing vegetables in brine (i.e., to make pickles). The French phrase dates from the 18th century, and was based on breadmaking, in which the French baker must deal with the sticky glop that eventually becomes a gorgeous baguette. If you've ever made the foolish decision to try to make your own bread, the metaphor should be obvious.

Have your cake and eat it too	Vouloir le beurre et
	l'argent du beurre
	(*To want the butter and the money*
	for the butter)

Though the English expression goes back well into the 1500s, sources indicate that the French one dates from the 19th century. But both of them describe an unrealistic desire, namely, to enjoy something and still retain it for additional pleasure. Thus, in the English version, the speaker wants to enjoy (eating) his cake, yet still have it to enjoy again; the French speaker wants to enjoy (selling) his butter, yet still have it to enjoy again. Although we give the English version in its most familiar form, this phrase has attracted considerable discussion. The issue is the implied sequence. Have your cake, and [then] eat it -- why should this be a problem? But if we reverse the order: eat your cake and [then] have it, we can clearly see the impossibility that is implicit in this old adage.[28]

---

[28] Wikipedia has an interesting (and humorous) article on the topic: https://en.wikipedia.org/wiki/You_can%27t_have_your_cake_and_eat_it

To be down in the dumps	Broyer du noir
	(*To grind the black*)

The English expression is not a reference to the holding place for garbage, but rather derives from the German adjective "dumpf," which originally meant "dulling the sight and hearing," but evolved into meaning dull, torpid, or heavy. The French expression most likely had its origins with the Renaissance painters, who had to grind up charred wood to make black paint. Given that black is the color of melancholy, it was a simple step for this phrase to refer to a gloomy mood.

Spread like wildfire	Se répandre comme une
	traînée de poudre
	(*Spread like a trail of powder*)

The French expression uses the image of a trail of gunpowder, often referred to as a cord of powder.

Be on tenterhooks	Être sur les charbons ardents
	(*Be on hot coals*)

The use of a wooden frame (a *tenter*) with small hooks protruding from its borders (*tenterhooks*) is a traditional way for housewives to keep sheets smooth and free from wrinkles as the clothes dry. It is less common today, but was a traditional tool for several centuries. It is an obvious leap to imagine that a person in some state of high anxiety might figuratively also be all stretched out, e.g., "on tenterhooks." The parallel French expression derives from the medieval torture chamber, where the victims would be forced to walk on burning coals; again, by analogy, someone in an anxious or disturbed state could figuratively be "on hot coals."

Crack a nut with a sledgehammer	Tirer sa poudre aux moineaux
	(*Shoot your rifle at the sparrows*)

The English expression, meaning to expend an enormous amount of effort to solve a small problem, apparently was first used in the mid-19th century in America. While the idiom here is probably the most common phrase, there are numerous other variants, e.g., use a hammer to kill a fly. The French expression, from the 17th century and now somewhat archaic, probably arose to criticize superfluous and excessive acts of gallantry.

Have a lump in your throat   Avoir un nœud dans la gorge
(Have a knot in your throat)

The French word 'nœud' is ultimately descended from the Latin nodus, 'node,' which primarily means a knot, but can also refer to a tie, a bond, a connection, or a crux. The French word continues the richness of meaning that it inherits; it can refer to knot, a tie, the bond of marriage, a friendly relationship, (and, in the vulgar argot, the tip of the penis). Next to that wealth of nuance, the English 'lump' seems rather feeble indeed. But we will return to this matter later...

Thick as thieves   S'entendre comme larrons en foire
(Get along like thieves at the fair)

The French expression goes back to the 16th century, and originally referred to dastardly men who collaborated as they stole; since they obviously plotted together, they obviously got along. The 17th century added the notion of stealing *at the fair*, not in the sense of a county fair, but rather any locale that was favored by numerous merchants hawking their wares. The English expression is somewhat more recent, and takes its imagery from an older meaning of "thick" to refer to individuals being densely packed together. Since groups of thieves were necessarily among such groups, the natural penchant for alliteration stepped in, and "thick as thieves" was the result.

Have a skeleton in the closet   Avoir une casserole à traîner
(Have a pan to drag)

The English expression dates from the early 19th century, and simply refers to having things in one's past that are embarrassing or hurtful should they be made known. One suggested origin for the expression was that doctors would secretly hide corpses for use in anatomical training, since that was not legal in the U.K until 1832. In any case, the expression is now "skeleton in the *cupboard*" in the U.K., while America retains the "closet" idea. The more colorful French phrase, meaning nearly the same thing, arose somewhat later, and derives from naughty children who attach a metal pan to a dog's tail. The poor animal is frightened by its clanging, and runs hither and yon (thus prolonging his agony). The French also made an exact copy of the English expression soon after it appeared in the 19th century: "Avoir un squelette dans le placard."

Twist someone around your little finger	Mener quelqu'un par bout du nez *(Lead someone by the tip of the nose)*

The French expression dates from about 1800, and means precisely what the English one does. The English expression is from roughly the same time; it began as "Twist someone around your finger." There is some question, unresolved as far as we could determine, about precisely when *little* entered the idiom.

Neither rhyme nor reason	Sans queue ni tête *(With neither tail nor head)*

The English expression, describing something illogical or meaningless, is very old; examples of it can be found in the 15th and 16th centuries. Shakespeare uses it both in *The Comedy of Errors:*

> Dromio: "Was there ever any man thus beaten out of season,
> When in the why and the wherefore is neither rhyme nor reason?
> Well, sir, I thank you."

and ten years later in *As You Like It:*

> Orlando: I swear to thee, youth, by the white hand of Rosalind, I
> am that he, that unfortunate he.
> Rosalind: But are you so much in love as your rhymes speak?
> Orlando: Neither rhyme nor reason can express how much.

The colorful French equivalent uses the notion of the head and the tail to represent the start and ending of a story; lacking these, the story is incomprehensible. We could not determine the origins of this phrase, but some sources indicate that it is relatively recent. Less colorful, but closer to the English is "Ça ne rime à rien" (that rhymes with nothing; that doesn't make sense).

Hit the jackpot	Decrocher la timbale *(Pick up the tympani)*

This French expression is probably a dilly for an English speaker, but like most expressions, makes sense when it is explained. First the English phrase. The term "jack-pot" arose in an early version of poker that flourished in the later 1800s, and in which, as in the present-day draw poker, a pair of jacks was needed to open. Eventually, the phrase began to be borrowed for winning at slot machines, which is its common usage today. For the French phrase, it's necessary to realize that the word "timbale" can mean the timpani, or kettle drum, of the classical orchestra. But it can also mean a silver goblet, which is its meaning here. The expression comes from country village festivals, where tall, greasy poles were erected, and packages of food were hung at the top, above which would hang a silver goblet. The stalwart climber who managed to slither his way to the top would win the goblet, i.e., hit the jackpot.

| Save up for a rainy day | Garder une poire pour la soif |
| | (*Save a pear for the thirst*) |

The French expression, meaning to save enough for the future, dates from the late 16th century, and is recorded in 1640 in a work by the linguist Antoine Oudin.[29] It uses the metaphor of keeping a juicy pear at hand by a traveler, for instance, who might be unable to easily find water. Balzac, in *The Lost Illusions,* has this wry statement about the idiom: "It is difficult to keep a pear for thirst, but it is more difficult, as you get older, to keep a thirst for the pear." The English expression is equally old; its first known use appears in the mid-16th century.

| A bunch of nobodies | Trois pelés et un tondu |
| | (*Three bald and one with short hair*) |

These rather cruel expressions are used to describe some collection of supposedly unimportant or uninteresting people that appear at some occasion or fail at some task.[30] It is also used to describe some event at which far fewer persons attend than expected. The English phrase is apparently timeless; we could find no sources that indicated any history of the phrase, and it has the feel of a contemporary coinage But since the French expression goes all the way back to Rabelais,[31] it is likely that there are some English antecedents lurking somewhere, though they stayed out of our searchlight. Rabelais' use of the word "pelé" possibly referred either to someone who was a scoundrel, or more likely

---

[29] (d. 1653)

[30] A nice example of turning this idiom on its head is "The Wikipedia Revolution: How A Bunch of Nobodies Created The World's Greatest Encyclopedia," Andrew Lih, 2009.

[31] François Rabelais. 1494-1553. French writer and humanist.

someone who had lost his hair due to illness. In similar fashion, his use of "tondu" (someone with short hair) probably referred to someone suffering from ringworm.

Read someone the riot act   Sonner les cloches (à quelqu'un)
                                      (*Ring the bells* [*at someone*])

The French phrase means reprimanding someone violently, the implicit nuance of violence coming from the extreme sound that a church bell would make were one to be too close to it; the expression dates from the 17th century. For the English expression, and surprisingly, the Riot Act really exists. In Great Britain during the early 18th century, there was a considerable amount of civil unrest; significant riots occurred in 1710 and 1714, with the result that Parliament passed a bill that was called "The Riot Act." It was aimed at preventing "rebellious riots and tumults," and gave policemen considerable authority to arrest; punishment for flouting the law could even include death. The Act was invoked on several occasions throughout the 18th and 19th centuries. The phrase began to be used figuratively in the early 19th century, and the Riot Act was eventually repealed in 1973.

(*And we can't leave without adding to the menagerie…*)

Holy cow   Ah, la vache

There is no clear explanation of the derivation of either expression, though it is indeed interesting that both languages would rely on a bovine image to express wonder or amazement, i.e., "Wow!" Some sources suggest that the French phrase goes back a few centuries; the English one is thought to have appeared later, in the early days of baseball. But nothing is certain. And why a cow?

My goose is cooked   Les carottes sont cuite
                                      (*The carrots are cooked*)

Both expressions have a fascinating history. For the French, and going back to the 17th century, "carottes,"because of a closeness of pronunciation at the time, had an unpleasant association with constipation. By the 19th century, the phrase had evolved into an equally curious implication that having your carrots cooked was to be dying. Only recently did this expression become a synonym for being in a hopeless state. For the English phrase, there is some debate as to the actual origin, but several sources attribute the phrase to the death of Jan Hus, a Czech priest in the early 14th century. His name resembled the Czech word "husa" ("goose") and he was burnt at the stake for heresy, so, figuratively speaking, his goose was cooked. An equivalent phrase in English is "I'm a dead duck."

Put a bug in the ear   Mettre la puce à l'oreille

An interesting expression, and largely the same in both languages. The French is quite old, and the English came directly from the French. Originally, it referred to a state of love or desire. In one of the fables of La Fontaine, we read: "The girl who thinks of her absent lover all night, so they say, with a flea in her ear." But soon after, the expression was transformed, and took on the notion of worry or agitation, and eventually got its current meaning of alerting someone of a forthcoming matter that is of some concern.

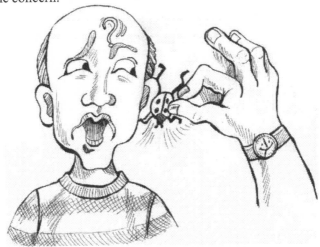

Fresh as *a daisy*   Frais comme *un gardon*
                                      (*Fresh like a roach*)

At first glance, a real doozy: what are these crazy Frenchmen thinking? But Frenchmen don't really think that icky bugs smell fresh. The roach (*Rutilus rutilus*) is a fresh fish of the Cyprinidae family, found throughout

Europe and western Asia. During the Middle Ages, when famines were common, fish were an important food commodity, and roaches were highly valued fish. Mystery solved.

Have goose pimples	Avoir la chair de poule
	(*Have the flesh of a chicken*)

Although apparently different, both phrases suggest that when one has a sudden fear or trembling, one's skin resembles that of a plucked fowl.

He's a book*worm*	C'est un *rat de bibliothèque*
	(*...library rat*)

The idiom makers in both languages must not be book lovers -- neither phrase is very pleasant, and neither worms nor rats are welcome visitors in most libraries.

Call *a spade a spade*	Appeler *un chat un chat*
	(*To call a cat a cat*)

Once again those pesky French cats!

Have pins and needles	Avoir des fourmis
	(*To have ants*)

Both expressions describe the tingling sensation that occurs when a lack of blood flow has reduced the normal sensations of some body part; another English phrase is "My leg (or arm, or foot) fell asleep." The French metaphor comes from the similarity of this unpleasant sensation to one where ants are crawling over that part of the body. Since the remedy is to move whichever limb has been affected, the phrase can also be extended to mean a need to move, and perhaps to leave wherever one is presently situated.

Blind as a *bat*	Aveugle comme une *taupe*
	(*...mole*)

Both animal images are of creatures that primarily live in darkness

(*To close this section, the following expression provoked an interesting excursion into French grammar...*)

Six of one, half-dozen of the other	C'est bonnet blanc et blanc bonnet
	(*It's a cap white and a white cap*)

The English phrase goes back at least to the late eighteenth century, as recorded in the journal of a British seaman. The French is somewhat older, and makes its point by inverting the order of the noun and adjective to arrive at the same meaning. But this simple phrase points out a key difference between the two languages. English adjectives **precede** the noun, except in rare cases that are usually either archaic or poetic, or appear in a very few standard clichés (e.g., time immemorial, heir apparent[32]).

French has a considerably more complex set of rules for adjective-noun order. In the simplest case, the adjective **follows** the noun, e.g., *le mot juste* (the right word). But a large number of very common adjectives **precede** the noun, including such everyday adjectives as those for: beautiful, good, short, tall, big, high, young, pretty, long, new, small, first, old, and so forth.

And some ornery French adjectives take on a different meaning (or at least a different nuance) depending on whether they precede or follow the noun, as in: *ma **propre** chambre* (my **own** bedroom), as compared to *la chambre **propre*** (the **clean** bedroom). Another example: *un **ancien** collègue* (a **former** colleague) as compared to: *un fauteuil **ancien*** (an **antique** chair).

Finally, there are several examples of really thorny either-or phrases which the novice French speaker should use at his peril: he should speak them **only** if he is absolutely sure which one he intends to mean: *une fille **petite*** (a small girl -- e.g., in size) vs. *une **petite** fille* (a little girl -- e.g., a child); *un **sacré** texte* (an impressive text – e.g., a new blockbuster novel) vs. *un texte **sacré*** (a sacred text–e.g., holy writ); and *un type **sale*** (a dirty person – e.g., someone who needs a shower) vs. *un **sale** type* (a foul person – e.g., someone without morals). *Bonne chance,* if you dare![33]

---

[32] There are also modern idiomatic uses of adjective-following order that most often concern indefinite pronouns, e.g., "someone strong." Wikipedia has an excellent article on the postpositive adjective: https://en.wikipedia.org/wiki/Postpositive_adjective

[33] A similar kind of switched meaning based on position can occur in English as well. Consider, for example, the contrasting meanings of "look over" and "overlook."

L'étalon-or/The gold standard

To end this little linguistic journey, we now look at some fascinating expressions where both languages go whole hog (!) at colorful and exotic imagery. It is interesting that, in many cases, these elaborate expressions describe very ordinary human situations.

Between a *rock* and a *hard place*	Entre le *marteau* et *l'enclume* (*Between a hammer and an anvil*)
Between the *devil* and the *deep blue sea*	Entre *l'arbre* et *l'écorce* (*Between the tree and the bark*)

All four of these idioms essentially describe the same situation, namely, being in a place one *really* does not want to be (and said far more evocatively in the English phrase, "Up shit creek without a paddle"). The idioms in the first pair are simple and descriptive: rock, hammer, hard place, anvil: no far-out metaphors here. However, the second pair provides far richer images. The origin of neither phrase is known, but in both cases, no explanation is necessary: each describes, in beautifully expressive terms, a difficult state where one must make a painful choice.

To be out of the picture	Être hors circuit (*To be outside of the circuit*)

The French phrase actually means to disconnect, or power down. Other figurative uses could be "out of commission," or "off the streets."

Hands down	Les doigts dans le nez (*The fingers in the nose*)

Both expressions originated in horse racing. The French describes a rider who is winning so easily, he can make a childish gesture of putting his finger in this nose. The English jockey merely drops his hands, relaxing his grip on the reins.

Wet your whistle   Rincer la dalle (*Rinse the slab*)

The English expression, where "whistle" is figuratively either one's lips
or throat, goes all the way back to Chaucer in *The Canterbury Tales*. For
the French phrase, the word "dalle" today means "paving stone" or "con-
crete slab." But before the sixteenth century the word "dalle" referred to a
channel through which water could pass. Hence, figuratively, the throat,
through which drinks must pass.

(*And since food also must take that same route...*)

I could eat a horse   Je pouvais crever la dalle
                                           (*I could burst the slab*)

The French phrase essentially means "I am starving." And "crever" is
one of those French words that just don't quite fit into English. The basic
meaning is "burst" or "puncture," but appears in many other meanings
(e.g., "Crève les yeux" – "Plain as the nose on your face," "Plutôt crever" –
"I'd rather die"). The English expression is pure hyperbole, and goes back
at least to the 1700s.

Throw in the towel   Jeter le manche après la cognée
                                           (*Throw the handle after the ax*)

Surprisingly, these two phrases have the same essential meaning. The
English expression comes from the world of boxing, where one fighter's
manager throws his towel into the ring when his man is hopelessly losing,
and must give up the fight. The French expression dates from the 14th or
15th century. According to legend, as a woodsman was once cutting down
a tree, the head of his ax came away from the shaft and flew into a deep
lake. Disappointed, and judging that he could never find his ax head, he
tossed the handle in as well, and gave up his task -- in other words, he
threw in the towel.

To have the *blues*   Avoir le *cafard*
                                      (*To have the cockroach*)

Both of these phrases are fascinating, though in very different ways. The French word "cafard" has several meanings. The term originated with the Arabic word "kafir," meaning "disbeliever" or "infidel." This then became a word for a hypocrite or deceitful person (compare the common English use of "rat"). It then became the name of the secretive little insect that scurries around a darkened room (and is the terror of a large number of otherwise mature adults). And finally, in the 19th century, Baudelaire[34] used "cafard" in *Fleurs du Mal* to connote a sense of sadness or melancholy. At roughly the same time, troops of the French Foreign Legion used it in the same manner; which of these sources was the true origin is not known. The English use of "blue" to denote depression or low spirits goes back to the 18th century. But it was the use of the term by composer W.C. Handy in the early 20th century that cemented the meaning of the phrase "to have the blues."

---

[34] Charles Baudelaire, French poet, 1821-1867.

(*Some interesting things about the French word bête*)

Bête (literally, "beast") is used in French in many interesting ways. For instance, the same phrase can mean quite different things, depending on who is being referred to:

C'est un bête noir (... *a black beast*)*:* If said of an abstract concept:, it means, roughly: That's my pet hate! But if said of a person, it means: I can't stand him!

It is often used have a more nuanced meaning, such as:
>Il est plus bête que mechant (*He is more beast than wicked*), which
>is properly translated as: *He's not really horrible, just stupid.*

And it can even take on meanings that appear to the English speaker as rather contrary:
>Bête comme chou! (*Beast like cabbage*) properly translated as:
>Easy as pie!

and
>Un bête de scéne (*Beast of scene*) A great performer

Send someone packing	Envoyer quelqu'un sur les roses
	(*Send someone on the roses*)

The thrust of the French expression is that if someone is extremely annoying, we should shove him into a rose bush hoping that he will suffer many pricks from the thorns of the flowers. The English phrases uses the verb "pack" with the meaning of leaving hurriedly, as if when sent away. This usage appears in Shakespeare's *Henry IV Part 1*, where Falstaff says: "Faith, and I'll send him packing."

Don't pull any punches	Ne pas y aller de main morte
	(*Don't go there with a dead hand*)

The French expression possibly dates from the 17th century, and simply refers to fighting with force, not with a limp fist. The English expression comes from boxing, where 'pulling' a punch is to hit an opponent with less than full force.

Be back at square one | Être Gros-Jean comme devant
(To be Gros-Jean like before)

"Gros-Jean" was a fictional boor; he was popularized by La Fontaine in the fable "La Laitière et le Pot au Lait." The expression means that even if you carefully give Gros-Jean instruction on some topic, he will understand it no better after hearing you, and you are right back to where you began. The English expression describes the state of returning to the beginning, though typically because of some failure. Its origin is disputed: one possible theory is from a children's board game, but a quite different theory argues that is started from football broadcasts in the 20th century. Alas, no matter how diligently we have searched, we are still back at square one....

Rule the roost | Faire la pluie et le beau temps
(Make the rain and good weather)

The French expression uses the image of having godlike power to govern the elements, hence, the ability to make important decisions and reward or punish others. It could equally well be translated by "Call the shots" or "Play first fiddle."

Once bitten, twice shy | Chat échaudé craint l'eau froide
(The scalded cat fears the cold water)

Instances of this saying go back to the Middle Ages. Both expressions imply that a victim of some grievous harm becomes doubly cautious, even when not warranted. Thus, since the cat knows that hot water will hurt (i.e., once bitten), he is equally afraid of cold water (i.e., twice shy).

He's not the sharpest knife in the drawer | Il n'a pas inventé l'eau chaude
(He didn't invent hot water)

Both languages are rich in idioms for this common mocking expression about someone's mental acuity; "il n'a pas inventé la poudre" ("he didn't invent powder"); "il n'a pas inventé le fil à couper le beurre" ("he didn't invent the butter knife"); "he's not the brightest bulb in the chandelier"; "he's a few cents short of a dollar"; and so forth.

Blood is thicker than water	La voix du sang est la plus forte (*The voice of the blood is the strongest*)

This expression offers a fascinating trip through antiquity. It is a corruption of "the blood of the covenant is thicker than the water of the womb," and some sources claim it is from a biblical phrase. It is indeed derived from Biblical material, but not apparently from a single phrase. Pastor Johnnie Akers[35] explains:

> During the ritual of ancient covenant making, the two parties involved would divide an animal in half, and stand together in the blood, with their right hands clasp[ed], and swear a mutual oath binding them to each other.... The relationship born of this union was so knit, that brothers made through the blood of covenants were closer to each other than brothers who were born from the same womb. Hence, blood (of the covenant) is thicker than water (of the womb).

This later came to be explained in several different ways, e.g., that blood shed by soldiers during battle provide a stronger bond than that of family, and other similar contexts.

A little bird told me	Mon petit doigt me l'a dit (*My little finger said it*)
The straw that breaks the camel's back	La goutte d'eau qui fait déborder le vase (*The drop of water that makes the vase overflow*)

The English expression goes back at least to 1677.[36] The French expression actually appears at roughly the same time, in the form of: "the last drop makes the cup run over."

---

[35] https://www.phrases.org.uk/bulletin_board/19/messages/141.html

[36] "It is the last feather that breaks the horse's back" (George Latimer Apperson, English Proverbs and Proverbial Phrases)

Out of the frying pan into the fire	Tomber de Charybde en Scylla *(Fall from Charybdis to Scylla)*

Charybdis and Scylla were two mythical sea monsters that Ulysses had to avoid during the Odyssey. The legend was that sailors who tried to avoid one would unfortunately find themselves in the arms of the other.

Have something up one's sleeve	Avoir plus d'un tour dans son sac *(Have more than one trick in your bag)*

Those wily French always assume that there's always at least one trick up one's sleeve; so this warns about someone's sleeve having two (or more!).

That's for the *birds*	C'est pour des *prunes* *(...for the plums)*

The French phrase originated during the Crusades. According to the legend, when the French soldiers went off to the Holy Land, they became enamored of the plums that grew there. The Crusade was a dismal failure, and when the soldiers returned, all they had to show for it was cuttings they had brought back from the plum trees. The King apparently was not amused, and was heard to exclaim "Don't tell me that's all they went for?" (i.e., if all they did was bring back some plums, the expedition was useless). The English expression is far more prosaic, and most likely emerged as military slang.

Spin a yarn	Raconter des salad *(To tell some salads)*

Just as adding lots of flavorful ingredients to fluff up a bland salad, adding a few humorous asides, inventing past events, and other flim-flam, can often make a tall story sound more believable. The origin of the English expression is debated, either coming from sailors or old maids; both, however, were occupied with spinning yarns, either of rope or fabric, and likely telling stories as they did it.

Pull the wool over someone's eyes   *Jeter de la poudre* aux yeux
                                                 (Throw the powder...)

Cost an *arm and a leg*   Coûter les *yeux de la tête*
                                                 (...the eyes of your head)

That takes the cake   C'est le comble
                                                 (That's the height)

The French word "comble" essentially refers to the extreme: the most, the limit. Thus, this expression could equally well be translated as "that's the last straw," "that beats everything," and other such English expressions.

To be a big hit   Faire un tabac
                                                 (To make tobacco)

In addition to meaning the plant, "tabac" also can refer to a beating (e.g., "passer quelq'un tabac" means to beat someone up), and by extension, to make a lot of noise. So one belief about this expression explains it as the sound of thunderous applause in the theatre, coming from a beating of the hands and feet.

Bite the hand that feeds you   Cracher dans la soupe
                                                 (Spit in the soup)

The origin of the French phrase is unclear, though it may have some resonance with the common British expression "To piss in someone's soup."

Beat around the bush   Tourner autour du pot
                                                 (To circle around the pot)

The English phrase originated in medieval hunting terminology: men were hired as beaters to scare a game animal out of its hiding place. But the beaters had to be careful not to beat on a bush or tree directly, since it might introduce an unwelcome new player (e.g., a swarm of bees) into the hunt; so they beat <u>around</u> it. In the French expression, "pot" refers to a large pot in which a meal for an entire family would be prepared. In times of scarcity, to "turn around the pot" was to try to sneak an extra bite or two without being noticed; later, the meaning evolved simply into "procrastinate."

A month of Sundays　　　　Une semaine de quatre jeudis
　　　　　　　　　　　　　　(*A week of four Thursdays*)

The French expression, although somewhat archaic now, dates from the end of the fifteenth century, originally in the form of "a week having two Thursdays." In the sixteenth, it became three Thursdays and finally became four. It refers to an impossible week, i.e., one that contains several identical days. The English phrase has the same essential meaning, though it is often used simply to connote 'a very long time'.

Make a mountain　　　　En faire tout un fromage
out of a molehill　　　　(*Make a whole cheese out of it*)

The English expression has many common forms, perhaps the most familiar one found in Shakespeare's title *Much Ado About Nothing*. The idiom as given here dates from the mid-sixteenth century, and in its first appearance, is given as an additional image to making an elephant out of a fly.

Have one foot in the grave　　　　Senter le sapin
　　　　　　　　　　　　　　(*To smell a fir tree*)

This expression dates from the 18th century. Since coffins were often made from fir trees, then figuratively, when one begins to realize that your days are numbered, it was said that you began to "feel the (fir) tree." There is also a more literal French version that closely mirrors the English: "avoir un pied dans la tombe" (Have a foot in the tomb.)

Lead someone up the garden path　　　Mener quelqu'un en bateau
　　　　　　　　　　　　　　　　(*Lead someone by boat*)

This odd French expression actually comes from confusion between the ancient word "bataleur" (a conjuror or trickster) and "batelier" (a boatman, one who drives a boat). Hence, the expression describes a deceiver who convinces someone of some false idea and leads him away, for some monetary or erotic gain. The English phrase, (sometimes using ...**down** the garden path) first appeared in print in 1926, in Ethel Mannin's *Sounding Brass*. The phrase was used to describe predatory women who, in order to seduce men, led them "up the garden." More interestingly, this term has been adopted by psycholinguists studying the effect on listeners of a "garden-path sentence" – a sentence that is grammatically correct, but is intentionally constructed to deceive the reader. A standard example is: "The old man the boat." Only after a frustrating few seconds does the reader realize that the sentence actually means: The old [are the ones who must] man the boat.

See which way the wind blows

Prendre le vent
(*Take the wind*)

Drink like a fish

Boire comme un templier
(*Drink like a Templar*)

The Templars were a Catholic military order founded in 1139 to protect pilgrims who journeyed to the Holy Land during the Crusades. The Templars were also prominent in the world of finance and became a wealthy and somewhat secretive group; as wealthy men, they had the reputation for, among other things, being mighty drinkers.

By hook or by crook

Coûte que coûte
(*Cost for cost*)

The English expression is very old, dating at least back to the writings of John Wycliffe (c. 1320-1384), English theologian and early protester against the Papacy. It essentially means using any actions necessary to accomplish a goal. The actual origin of the phrase is debated, and is ascribed variously to names of locations in Ireland (the Hook Peninsula and the village of Crook), or the ancient practice of peasants gathering firewood (picking up dead or fallen branches using a sharpened hook and a shepherd's crook). Unlike the English expression, we could find no data on the origin of its French parallel. But we will keep searching and will find an answer, by hook or by crook!

Give up the ghost   Passer l'arme à gauche
                                     (*Pass the weapon to the left*)

Both of these idioms are descriptions of death, The English phrase dates at least back to the 17th century, in the King James Bible (published in 1611): 'Jesus... gave up the ghost.' Mark 15:37. (Note that the parallel passage in Matthew is "Jesus ...*yielded* up the ghost.") The more likely term that would be used today would be "spirit," in the same way that the traditional name "Holy Ghost" is now often replaced by "Holy Spirit," which is a more exact translation of the Latin *Sancte Spiritus*. The French expression is a far more complex problem in etymology. There have been many origins suggested, including fencing (where the primacy of the right hand is critical), military practice (the rifle sits on the left foot when the soldier is at rest), and the medieval practice of moving a husband's coat of arms to the left of his widow's when he dies). The one that seemed most appropriate to us was an ascription from the Napoleonic era: when a soldier had to reload his rifle, he held it in his left hand while he searched for more bullets with his right, thus exposing himself to enemy fire. This would then relate this idiom to one from 20th century warfare: "three on a match" was unlucky because it would give enough time for an enemy sniper to zero in and kill the third soldier lighting his cigarette.

Tear into someone   Tirer à boulets rouges
                                     (*Shoot red cannonballs at someone*)

The "red" in the French expression refers to fire, i.e., the cannonballs would be flaming. Thus, the expression, from the 18th century, suggests an extremely violent attack on someone. Similarly, the English expression means to make a violent criticism or rebuke of someone; its origin is not clear, though it is very likely rather recent.

Go from pillar to post   Aller de Caïphe a Pilate
                                (*Go from Caiphas to Pilate*)

Both phrases connote a ceaseless wandering back and forth with little result; both are quite old. The French expression uses a metaphor from the Gospel stories, in which Christ was brought between Caiphas, the High Priest, and Pontius Pilate, the Roman governor of Judaea (and then to Herod and then back to Pilate). The English expression is the source of considerable disagreement. One train of thought is that the "pillar and "post" refer to the pillars and posts of a tennis court. Another suggestion is that it is derived from the punishment of criminals; whipped at a whipping post and then placed in the pillory to be publically humiliated. It was at this point that your humble authors wished that they had ignored "Go from pillar to post," and had chosen "Go hither and yon" instead.

Go through the mill   Avaler des poires d'angoisse
                             (*Swallow pears of anxiety*)

Each of these curious expressions refers to undergoing significant hardship, enduring severe pain or discomfort, or other gruesome and horrible conditions. The French phrase is far older, dating back to the torture chambers of medieval times, when anyone who was anybody just **had** to have a torture chamber of his own. When putting some poor wretch through his paces, so to speak, there was often a good deal of loud screaming, and to minimize these unpleasant sounds, the torturer would insert a spring-based device, which had the shape of a pear, into the victim's mouth, and voila, the screaming was stifled -- problem solved! The English expression, slightly less gory, dates from the 19th century, and uses the image of grinding down grain as a metaphor for enduring some painful or trying experience.

At daybreak   À pointe du jour
                     (*At the tip of the day*)

It's curious that in English, day *breaks,* but night *falls.* The French echo the latter exactly -- nightfall is "La nuit tombe." But the French also have a quite different and very beautiful word for the start of the day: "l'aube," which corresponds to English "dawn."

Be ignored; be talking to a wall	Se prendre un vent (*Take to one's self a wind*)

The French expression is probably relatively recent, and plays upon the image of a man who approaches the face of another for a kiss, but when the other suddenly withdraws, it is only the wind that kisses his face.

Pull someone's leg	Mettre quelqu'un en boîte (*Put someone in a box*)

Dressed to the nines	Se mettre sur son trente-et-un (*To put on your thirty-one*)

The etymology of both of these expressions is unclear. For the English phrase, as early as the 18th century, "to the nines" related to excellence or perfection, but how it came to be related to clothing is not known; an equivalent English expression "Wearing your Sunday clothes" is considerably more obvious. While the origin of the French phrase is equally unclear, one belief is that it refers to December 31, i.e., referring to someone who is dressing up to greet the New Year.

Nip something in the bud	Étouffer quelque chose dans l'oeuf (*Choke something in the egg*)

Both phrases figuratively describe preventing something young or small from growing larger. The English is likely based on a late frost that kills young flowers; it is at least as old as the early 17th century. The origin of the French expression is unknown, but obviously refers to the same idea as does the English.

Born yesterday	Né de la derniere pluie (*Born of the last rain*)

The "last rain" connotes something that is recent or fresh, hence innocent and inexperienced.

'Till the cows come home	Jusq' à la saint-glinglin (*Until Saint Glinglin*)

There are various explanations for the English phrase, most of them descriptive of the languid behavior of cows, which sometimes do not return to the stable for long periods, or even, should they become lost, never. For the French phrase, "Glinglin" is a corruption, from the Metz region of France, of the German word "Klingen," meaning to ring or resound. It became metaphorically associated with a nonsensical ringing of a bell for the feast of a nonexistent saint and took on the meaning of something that could never occur.

| Blow your top | Sortir de ses gonds |
| | (*Leave your hinges*) |

In English, "Blow your top," meaning to lose your temper, is obviously a metaphor for a closed container of liquid being heated to the point that its cap explosively shoots off. The French expression, "Leave your hinges," becomes a little closer to English when we consider that from the sixteenth century, the English expression "get out of one's hinges" was used as a common description of an individual who was unstable, or behaving in an confused manner. And to this day, the expression "Come unhinged" means to become angered or crazed; to lose control of one's senses or sanity: in other words, to blow your top!

(*And the inevitable parade of beasties...*)

| Be like a bee in clover | Être comme un coq en pâte |
| | (*Be like a rooster in paste*) |

The essential English expression is "in clover," though it can often be seen as "high clover" or "tall clover." It comes, at least partly, from the preference of cows for grazing on clover. There are several related phrases – bee in clover, pig in clover – and all connote being in a state of contentment. The French expression is quite old and is actually two idioms in one. The original form, dating from well before the 17th century, was of a "coq au panier" (rooster in a basket) which describes a rooster being taken to sell at the market. To insure the highest price, the bird would be carefully placed in a basket to show off how well fed it was. In the 17th century, however, the reference to "panier" (basket) was replaced by "pâte" (paste), and exactly what was meant is in dispute. One thought is that 'paste' described the poor bird after it had been slaughtered, and had been made into a tasty paste (i.e., pâté). The other is that 'paste' refers to some oily substance rubbed into the poor bird's wings to make them shine. Whichever is true, the poor rooster was going to end up in the stew pot, come what may.

Be a guinea pig   Servir de cobaye

The interesting aspect of this pair is that both refer to the same animal. The French word "cobaye" is the proper zoological term for a rodent found in the Andes, and named Cavia Cobaya. The English name is doubly fanciful, since it is neither a pig nor from Guinea. But both languages now reflect the common use of these poor animals in scientific research.

When pigs fly   Quand les poules
auront des dents
(*When hens have teeth*)

Buy a *pig* in a *poke*   Acheter *chat* en *poche*
(*To buy a cat in a bag*)

In the English expression, the word "poke" actually began as a French word meaning "small bag," and eventually evolved into the English word "pocket." The word "poke" still survives in Scotland as either "pok" or "pock," meaning bag, wallet, or sack. The French expression dates from the fifteenth century and shows again the French preference for cats in their idioms.

Ugly as *sin*   Laid comme un *pou*
(*Ugly like a louse*)

The French win the metaphor prize with this one, because while it's not clear whether or not anyone has actually seen a sin, there's no doubt that one can see lice, and they are **really** ugly…

Cat got your tongue   Donner sa langue au chat
(*Give your tongue to the cat*)

Both have the general meaning of being silent when one is expected to speak. The origin of the English expression is unknown, though it may have come directly from the French. The French expression can also be voiced as "chat a ta langue". But it is interesting that, finally, both languages agree to use the imagery of a cat to make the same point.

Raining cats and dogs   Il tombe des hallebards
(Halbards are falling)

There are apparently no explanations for the English phrase; many theories have been propounded, but none have been accepted as definitive. For the French phrase, a halbard is an ancient form of military lance, and Gaston Esnault, a 19th century lexicographer and authority on slang, reports that the word "lance" eventually became a slang word for water, and especially rainwater. An earthier French expression for the same concept is: "pleuvoir comme une vache qui pisse" ("to rain like a pissing cow").

Fight like cats and dogs   Se battre comme des *chiffonniers*
(...scavengers)

The French expression dates from the period when paper was made from old rags, and the scavengers sought out (and doubtless fought over) any discarded rags and sold them to paper manufacturers.

I have other *fish to fry*   J'ai d'autres *chats a fouetter*
(... cats to whip)[37]

Those poor French cats...Both phrases refer to having more important things to do. The idioms differ only in that the French prefer whipping cats to frying fish.

---

[37] DC: Some sources give the expression as "...autres <u>chiens</u> a fouetter (other <u>dogs</u> to whip). But both HCR and ERI say <u>cats</u>, and so does Ben; hence, so do I.

However, and speaking of cats: we earlier saw how the French made the English look pretty feeble when comparing our flimsy "lump" expression with their far richer word "nœud," a metaphor that combined images of a knot, a tie, a marriage bond, and even the tip of the penis.

So, to even things up, and as a fitting conclusion...

Have a *frog* in the throat
Avoir un *chat dans* la gorge
(*...cat in the throat*)

Various attempts have been made to trace this 19th century English expression to bizarre practices of medieval doctors, but such attempts are, in all likelihood, without merit. The phrase has nothing exotic about it: when you have a frog in the throat, you simply sound like a frog. The French expression is considerably older, apparently arising from a pun between the word "maton," meaning a clump of curdled milk, and "chat," the proper word for cat.

But whatever else is true, the honors are now even between the two languages for the glorious imagery of each idiom. And, risking some Gallic criticism, wouldn't one think that the above images could be switched?

Afterword

Dear friends,

Now we have finished our little trip through the weird, wacky, and wonderful world of idioms. So it's time to cease and desist, give it a rest, call it a day, cash in the chips, and hang it all up. Thank you all for giving us a read!

David & Ben

Envoi

Chers amis,

Cette fois, les carottes sont cuites, c'est la fin des haricots, et malgré un p'tit goût de trop peu, nous tirons notre révérence, on file, on se taille, on se fait la belle. Merci de nous avoir lus !

Ben & David

About the Authors

 David Carney was born in 1942, and attended college at the Catholic University of America, receiving a Bachelor's degree in music theory. He received a Master's degree from the University of Southern California, after which he served on the faculty of the Oberlin Conservatory. He later lived in Boston, where he served as assistant organist at King's Chapel, and also was Assistant Conductor of the Handel & Haydn Society, and harpsichordist of the Boston Classical Orchestra. During this period, he also received his Doctorate in Music Theory, and served on the music faculty at Boston University, In 1980, his career underwent a significant change, and he completed studies at Boston University for a Master of Science degree in Computer Science. Subsequent to that, he worked as a computer programmer for Intermetrics, Inc., and later was a Research Staff Member at the Institute for Defense Analyses in Alexandria, VA. He then accepted a position on the staff at Carnegie Mellon's Software Engineering Institute in Pittsburgh, PA. After retiring, he moved to Santa Fe, NM, and presently lives in Palm Springs, CA. His interest in the French language has been lifelong; he is presently working on a French-ScottishLexicon.

djc717@gmail.com